STAGE STRUCK

Published to coincide with its West End première, **Stage Struck** is a macabre comedy-thriller by the author of *Butley, Otherwise Engaged, The Rear Column* and *Close of Play.*

In his younger days, Robert Simon was a first-rate stage-manager in provincial rep.. Now he keeps house for his West End actress wife, while amusing himself with lots of little sexual adventures. In fact, a thoroughly happy man. Until one evening, through the clumsy intervention of a psychiatrist, his happiness and his marriage are destroyed. He plans a hideous revenge, both on his wife and on the psychiatrist . . . a revenge which allows him to rediscover all his old talents.

Simon Gray

STAGE STRUCK

EYRE METHUEN · LONDON

First published in Great Britain in 1979 by Eyre Methuen Ltd,
11 New Fetter Lane, London EC4P 4EE
Copyright © 1979 by Simon Gray
Set in IBM 10pt. Journal by 7\Tek-Art, Croydon, Surrey
Printed in Great Britain by Whitstable Litho Ltd.,
Whitstable, Kent.

ISBN 413 46970 0 (Paperback)

At the time of going to press, **Stage Struck** was scheduled for first production by Michael Codron at the Vaudeville Theatre, London, on 20 November 1979, with the following cast:

ROBERT	Alan Bates
HERMAN	Andrew Sharp
ANNE	Sheila Ballantine
WIDDECOMBE	Nigel Stock

Directed by Stephen Hollis
Designed by Carl Toms

Note
During rehearsal for the first production, the author wrote an additional passage of dialogue for Robert and Anne in Act One Scene One. It appears in this edition as an Appendix after the play.

ACT ONE

Scene One

The living-room of a large house in the country, not far from London. Say, between London and Brighton. It is an old farm-house, modernised but not too radically converted. Stage right there are french windows. Stage left a door that leads to the hall, front door, and stairs to the upstairs part of the house. Stage back, an arch that leads to the kitchen. The walls of the room are panelled, rectangularly from three-quarters of the way up, down to the floor; and in large squares above. One of these squares, in the middle, is in fact a concealed opening to a large cupboard or bidey-hole — originally, perhaps, the entrance to a loft. There is another one directly opposite, but not of course visible to the audience.

The furnishing in the room consists of a desk near the french windows (stage right), several arm-chairs and a sofa, a small table, a drinks side-board, etc; There are books in book-shelves, some to do with the theatre and its history, others complicated do-it-yourself books. There is also the odd poster for plays, featuring ANNE ROBERTS *from under to above the title. There is a telephone on the desk. There is a ladder against the wall, built so that it blends against it, which leads to the cubby-hole panel. A rope pulls the panel open. When the curtain goes up it is late evening, in summer. The french windows are open. The cubby-hole panel is open. There is a pile of magazines, Stage, Plays and Players, etc: at the foot of the ladder.* ROBERT *appears from the loft, scales nimbly down the ladder, humming. Picks up the pile, goes on up the ladder. Goes into the cubby-hole.*

HERMAN *appears through the french windows. He is carrying a gun, looking thoughtful. He looks around, makes to go towards the kitchen.* ROBERT *reappears at the top of the ladder, begins to come down.* HERMAN *sees him. He hesitates, then slips the gun back into his pocket.*

ROBERT (pushing the ladder against the wall). Oh, hello Herman. How are you.

HERMAN *shrugs.*

ROBERT. Working hard?

HERMAN. Well, I haven't done much recently. For one thing I can't get to the library. On Monday there was the tube strike. Then on Tuesday the library porters were on strike so they wouldn't fetch any books up, then on Wednesday the librarians came out to show solidarity with the porters who'd gone back and then yesterday when I telephoned to find out what was going on nobody answered, so I suppose the telephonists were out to show solidarity with the librarians who've probably gone back.

ROBERT. What I'm looking forward to is a tourists' strike, a day when they'll all refuse to come out of their hotels and spend their money looking at our pagentry and picket-lines, so I can go into town and do some exotic shopping without being treated as an undesirable resident, eh, drink?

HERMAN. No thanks.

ROBERT. Oh. Are you all right. You look a bit low.

HERMAN. Do I? Perhaps because it all seems to bloody pointless.

ROBERT. Oh it is, from what I can make out. Because apparently the money they finally get is worth less than the money they were getting when they went on strike for it by the time they actually suceed in getting it which is why they have to come out again immediately they've got it to get some more of it and so forth, don't worry about it and do have a drink.

HERMAN. No, I was talking about my thesis. It doesn't matter to me whether I get on with it or not. (*He sits down.*)

ROBERT. Poor old Henry James, oh that reminds me, I've forgotten to let the wine breathe. (*Taking a bottle out of the cupboard, checking the label, replacing it with another of something different.*) I've got a little pheasant in the oven, a very little one, sadly won't go around for three, or I'd ask you to stay on to dinner again.

HERMAN. Do you want me to go?

ROBERT. No no, of course not, I say aren't you a mite touchy
for you, at least wait and say hello to Anne, she shouldn't be
too long now they've persuaded her leading man to cut down
on his curtain calls, and then push off if you feel *de trop*.
(*As he puts out knives and forks rapidly on the table.*) But
excuse me if I just — so we can start as soon as Anne gets
back, she's always peckish — there — (*Turns, looks at*
HERMAN.) I say, you really do look subdued, what have you
been up to?

HERMAN. Tell me something, Robert.

ROBERT. Yes?

HERMAN. What do you think of me?

ROBERT. What?

HERMAN. What do you really think of me. Straight out.

ROBERT. Straight out?

HERMAN. Yes.

ROBERT. Well, I don't know, Herman, I haven't thought too
much about you. But we're both delighted you've taken over
the cottage, and not simply because you're a guaranteed short-
term tenant, and I do enjoy your little droppings-in and just-
passings-by when I'm on my own, if that means anything.

HERMAN. But you do think there's something odd about me,
don't you? I've noticed the smiles you give Anne sometimes
when I say something.

ROBERT. I'm sorry. I never meant you to notice them.

HERMAN. But what do you say about me when my back is
turned?

ROBERT. Well, nothing really cruel Herman, I promise, none of
the current round of anti-antipodean jokes, it's all very
affectionate. And some of your little gestures have touched
Anne quite deeply, you know. The note and flowers you sent
her for getting you a ticket to her play, for instance. Although
while we're on the subject I should perhaps take the

opportunity of warning you against lilies for actresses, even sensible ones like Anne are superstitious.

HERMAN. What, do they mean bad luck?

ROBERT. Well, death, usually. I must tell you all about actors' superstitions, whistleing, Macbeth, green, there was an old ham I used to know in Worthing who'd worked with Wolfitt —

HERMAN. In other words, I'm what you'd call gauche, right?

ROBERT. Naive, I'd call it, Refreshingly naive.

HERMAN. Let's face it, Robert, I'm a hick.

ROBERT. Herman, I believe you're suffering from delayed culture shock.

HERMAN. Right. I am. Because I'm in love, you see.

ROBERT. Ah. Ah hah. Who with?

HERMAN. Griselda.

ROBERT. Griselda, eh? Well — well, that's a very nice name. And with a built-in defence against diminutives. Well, that's good news, Herman.

HERMAN. Is it? She's married.

ROBERT. Oh. Who to?

HERMAN. Some man or other.

ROBERT. Well, that certainly narrows the field.

HERMAN. Gris won't talk about him. Except to say she doesn't love him any longer, and she hasn't for years but he doesn't know it.

ROBERT. Still, she's already told you more about him than he knows himself.

HERMAN. The poor bastard thinks he's blissfully married. And he thinks she is too. Even though he's been unfaithful to her right from the beginning almost. Seven years. So really he's got it coming to him, hasn't he? I can see that. But then why do I feel such a — a shit.

ROBERT. It does you credit. No pommy of your age would feel

a shit in those circumstances, I can tell you.

HERMAN. That's what Gris keeps saying. She thinks I'm being naive too, at least until last night she did.

ROBERT. Why, what did you do last night?

HERMAN. Well, she came around to the cottage — hey, I hope you don't mind my having her in the cottage.

ROBERT. Good God, Herman, you have her where you can.

HERMAN. Thanks Robert. And afterwards I tried to make her understand what I felt about what we were doing, and suddenly she turned really nasty. She said I was like a convict.

ROBERT. Oh good Heavens, that's a simple matter of togs and letting your hair grow —

HERMAN. She was talking about my post-coital guilt. She said I looked so guilty and beaten and ashamed, and I said, I can't help it, that's how I do feel, and I can't see how you don't feel the same way. And she said, the trouble is, I'm not good enough for a hick like you, and she walked out.

ROBERT. Oh dear.

HERMAN. It'd be all right if she married me. I know it would.

ROBERT. Married you?

HERMAN. Right.

ROBERT. Well — look, have she and — some man — any children?

HERMAN. Two little boys.

ROBERT. Well, that does complicate things. They can be a dreadful nuisance, especially in divorce proceedings. I remember one of Anne's friends, she played Laerta to Anne's Hamlet in the all-female a few years back, by the way, had a nightmare time of it over the custody of their twins. Her husband fought her at every turn.

HERMAN. But she won in the end, I hope!

ROBERT. Oh yes. He had to keep them. But she has to do a few weeks every Christmas and Easter and Summer.

HERMAN. But I wouldn't mind her having them, I love kiddies.

ROBERT. Do you really? Well, what about her, does she want to marry you?

HERMAN. She's said so, once or twice. Until last night.

ROBERT. Oh, last night was just a lovers' tiff, really Herman, I can't see your problem.

HERMAN. The husband, of course. What about him, the poor bastard!

ROBERT. Oh, good God Herman, you really are being a little over-scrupulous there, you know. I mean, a) he's not a friend of yours, b) she doesn't love him, c) he's been consistently unfaithful to her —

HERMAN. What's that got to do with it? What about you and Anne?

ROBERT. Mmmm?

HERMAN. Well, you and Anne lead pretty free sexual lives, don't you?

ROBERT. Anne's reputation is absolutely spotless. Even in the Green Room almost. Why recently she's been receiving soliciting letters from the Gay Liberation Front. Really Herman, I don't want to come the heavy hubby, but I'd really rather you kept Anne out of this.

HERMAN. What about you then?

ROBERT. What about me?

HERMAN. Well, a couple of nights ago when I dropped in you told me a story about a girl you had a fling with you called it when you were stage-managing somewhere in Yorkshire and then from something Anne said over supper I worked out afterwards you and Anne must actually have been married at the time.

ROBERT. Whatever you do, Herman, you mustn't abandon research, you've got a nose for it. (*Little pause.*) Well. So what?

HERMAN. So. Suppose I came along to you and said too bad, old son, I'm taking your Anne away from you.

ROBERT *laughs.*

HERMAN. What would you do?

ROBERT. I hope — *(Recovering himself.)* — I'd have the grace to accept it.

HERMAN. Would you truly? So you're telling me to go ahead then, Robert, and to Hell with the consequences.

ROBERT. Under the circumstances, I can't think of a better place for them.

HERMAN *takes the gun out of his pocket, very slowly. Points it at* ROBERT.

There is a pause.

ROBERT. Is that loaded?

HERMAN. Right.

ROBERT. With live bullets?

HERMAN. Right.

ROBERT. Well Herman — *(Laughs nervously.)* — I'm sorry if my — my — my advice hasn't been on the right moral lines but — but we're probably confronted here with a classic case of culture gap, aren't we. In the old country we don't pull guns on people whose advice we disagree with, especially when it's offered in the best of faith. *(Pause.)* If I've once or twice seemed to be frivolous about your problem please forgive me, I picked up some rather unattractive habits during my years in — in rep. *(Pause.)* Sorry.

HERMAN. What?

ROBERT. I'm apologising.

HERMAN. What for, Robert?

ROBERT. Whatever you're pointing that thing at me for.

HERMAN. What, oh sorry, Jesus, did you think I was going to shoot you? No. It's from her, from Gris. You see, this afternoon I went out for a walk, to try and get things clear in my mind about her walking out last night, and to keep away from the telephone, because I promised her I'd never 'phone her at home in case he was there, and when I got back this was on my pillow, no, on her side of our pillow, no message with it, I haven't done a year's post-graduate on Henry James without being able to interpret a symbol when I see one! But what does it mean, Robert? What does it mean?

ROBERT. Are you sure your Griselda is English, this has more than a touch of the Teutonics or Scandinavians about it, can I see it. (*He Takes it from* HERMAN, *hand trembling, opens it, looks in it.*) Yes, live all right, like old times, the number of Agatha Christies and so forth I've had to handle these in, or had them pointed at me and been shot at and killed by with blanks of course, (*Laughs.*) or keep them loaded up for the last scene of *Gabler,* three different productions and in two of them I longed for live ammunition, given the ladies in question, Anne was a superb Hedda by the way, even though not quite ready for it, the truth is Herman, the truth is that the old cliché holds true, never, never, never point these things at people, particularly when loaded —

There is the sound of a car, off, left.

ROBERT. Oh, there's Anne, put it away, she hates the things, even on stage. (*He gives it to* HERMAN.)

HERMAN. Don't tell her, will you. About Gris and me.

ROBERT. Really? Why not?

HERMAN. I just don't want her to know. I respect her too much, and I'd feel treacherous to Gris, too, letting another woman in on it. So please —

ROBERT. All right.

HERMAN. Promise.

ROBERT (*laughing*). I promise.

ANNE *enters, carrying carrier bags etc.*

ROBERT. Hello darling, you've timed it bang on for the pheasant, how did it go?

ANNE. Bloody quickly, that's how it went. That bugger Tom cut into every single one of my lines, even when I was announcing the suicide, he rattled straight in as if I'd said she's put the chicken in the oven and not her head, so it went for nothing, my only real moment in the play, and when I asked him afterwards what the hell he thought he was up to, he said, well darling, if we're all so desperate for our din-dins we're not allowed a decent curtain, and I said it wasn't din-dins it was just that the rest of us didn't particularly enjoy going on bowing after the audience had stopped clapping.

ROBERT. What sort of house?

ANNE. Seventy-five per cent.

ROBERT. Well darling, that's really not bad for a Tuesday night considering it's not a comedy or a musical or a thriller or even much of a play, so it must be you, darling, packing them in.

ANNE. From the response at the end what we're mainly packing in is the Japs and the raincoats for the two-minute nude scene, Alice's tits looked really weird tonight. I think she's been oiling them, every time her nipples caught the light they sort of winked at me — oh, and there was my usual couple in the front row, 'she's not as pretty as her picture, is she' 'no, and why that dreadful wig!'

HERMAN. Well, you know what I think, Anne, I think you're just great in it. Just great!

ANNE. Oh hello Herman, who is she?

HERMAN. Who?

ANNE. The lady who was letting herself into the cottage just now as I passed.

HERMAN. Oh — oh yes, I'd forgotten she was coming over, just a friend, Anne, a research student too, well I'd better get down there — well thanks, Robert, thanks for everything, goodnight both. (*He goes out through the french windows.*)

ROBERT. What did she look like?

ANNE. Blonde and dumpy, as far as I could make out. Who is she?

ROBERT (*who has been mixing a drink*). Ah, well, I'm afraid I promised Herman I wouldn't tell you that her name's Gris, for

Griselda, he wants to marry her, she might want to marry him, but he's conscience-stricken about her husband and two children, so she sent him a loaded gun symbolically which he then drew on me. I think that's everything I promised not to tell you, sorry darling.

ANNE. A loaded gun?

ROBERT. Yes, I'll tell you while we're noshing, scared me shitless but it was really quite funny, just like the time at Worthing when I realised just as you were squeezing the trigger I'd forgotten to put the blanks in, remember, hang on while I check the pheasant. (*He goes into the kitchen.*)

ANNE *sits for a moment, then takes out a cigarette. Her hand is trembling slightly. She looks at it, slaps it. Lights the cigarette, hand steady.*

ROBERT (*re-enters, carrying a salad bowl, condiments*). Perfect. As soon as you've finished your one fag — oh, by the way, no fresh vegetables because of the trucker's strike, or seed strike, or sun strike, whichever, but I've had a lettuce thawing out of the freezer, we must remember to stock up, we're running low, I'm doing Italian for a change, O.K.

ANNE. Actually, I'm not very hungry.

ROBERT. You didn't have a sandwich — or one of those sodding yoghurts?

ANNE. No. I'm just not up to one of your elaborate meals.

ROBERT (*looks at her, makes as if to say something, checks himself*). Look darling, I can see you're tired and past it (*Goes to her, takes her hands*) and that swine Tom cutting your lines, we'll find a lovely way to strike back, and there's nothing wrong with your wig —

ANNE. Yes, there is.

ROBERT. Well, a bit rat-tailey perhaps, the last time I saw it, tomorrow morning we'll make smashing fusses on the telephone and screw another one out of Michael but what you need now my love is a proper meal and bed, eh?

ANNE. Oh, for God's sakes, don't baby-talk me.

ROBERT. Baby-talk you!

ANNE. You were almost lisping, it was revolting.

ROBERT. Sorry. I was merely trying to get you to the table and some food down you — and perhaps I'm a bit peckish myself, you know, I did spend the afternoon moving all your unwanted magazines into the loft and the evening doing my best to get a meal you'd enjoy — and I asked you if you'd like pheasant —

ANNE *groans.*

ROBERT. What?

ANNE. Now it's the put-upon housewife.

There is a pause.

ANNE. I'm sorry. That's not how I meant to start. We've got to talk darling.

ROBERT. What about?

ANNE. You mainly. And me. Our marriage.

ROBERT. But — but what about the — the pheasant.

ANNE (*looks at him*). Oh God, Robert.

ROBERT (*sits down*). All right. Where do we begin — with me mainly or you or our marriage. I mean, we've been perfectly happily married for seven years without having to talk about it, which is perhaps why it's been a perfectly happy marriage, while all our friends have been analysing and fretting their way to divorce courts and shrinks and so forth.

ANNE. It's never been a perfect marriage. From the beginning. Or why have you had to have all those affairs?

ROBERT. What affairs?

ANNE. Oh Robert, I've always known — right from the days in rep. with those little scrubbers in jeans and vests and Caroline Wycherley and Hazel Montague and on and on — you're a lousy adulterer. An insultingly lousy adulterer, you must be the only man in the western world, darling, who lays girls with smeary lip-stick, on your handkerchiefs and your shirt-fronts

and even on your Y-fronts, once, just like a husband in an old
Susan Hayward movie — and your habit of coming to bed
without taking a bath, smelling as if you had, which means you
must have without my knowing, and perfumes and hairs on
your jackets and — oh good God, darling, all those wrong-
number 'phone calls or stilted conversations with your new
agent or somebody you said wanted to be your agent, which
were totally meaningless from what you let me hear of them
from your end, but always involved lunch arrangements which
weren't. Meaningless, I mean, as that's what the calls were
about. I can always tell when you're lying, you see, darling,
you do it in such a reppy style, and look so pleased with
yourself for having got away with it — why, you even 'phone
them up when I'm in the room, don't you, I expect it gives
you quite a thrill, nodding and smiling at me as you pretend
to be taking a strong line with some script-editor while you're
actually fixing up a fuck with his weak little secretary or
whoever, how she must have admired your nerve, eh, and
laughed at me, and brought back your great days in Worthing,
and that's the only thing I've really had against it recently, in
the end, your taste. (*Pause.*) So you see darling, I do know,
Really.

ROBERT. And yet you let me go on and on — without saying a
thing, without even hinting or looking upset —

ANNE. Oh yes, it's been partly my fault. I see that now. I blame
myself. I put up with it because I thought you must need it —
because I was making a career and you weren't, and if it hadn't
been for me and the money I was beginning to make you'd
never have given up stage managing, which you were so good
at, and concentrated on your acting —

ROBERT. Which I wasn't.

ANNE. You were all right.

ROBERT. I was bloody better than all right, and you know it! I
was offered lots of things, they simply weren't worth my
while.

ANNE. I know. And I blamed myself for that, too. If it hadn't

been for me you'd have had to take them. And one thing
might have led to another —

ROBERT. Yes, one sten-gun carrier to another in those
Shakespeares at the R.S.C., or one P.C. at Brighton to another
at Croydon — I gave them a chance, I was killed seven times
on television in my last year of work — seven times killed for
one and a half minutes' exposure. And four of those times my
face wasn't visible. I wore a beard, a stocking-mask, heavy
scar-tissues —

ANNE. I know, I know. I'm not blaming you.

ROBERT. You're accusing me of living off your money.

ANNE. Well, you are.

ROBERT. But you've always insisted on calling it our money.
Whenever I've objected to your paying some of the bills —

ANNE. All the bills darling. These last few years. And you didn't
object to my paying them, simply at your not being able to
pay them.

ROBERT. Yes, well you're one of those people whose talent is
recognised and who get rewarded for it too. I'm not. And if
it hadn't been for me, supporting you, running our lives —
who chose this house, who furnished it, keeps it going, cooks
the meals — how would you have managed without any of
that, eh?

ANNE. Oh yes. I know all that you've done. And why. I was
just explaining to you why I let your affairs go on and on. It
was because I thought you needed them when you were just a
stage-manager, to make up for not being an actor, and that you
needed them when you tried to make a go of it as an actor to
make up for not making a go of it, and that you've gone on
having them to make up for not making a go of it as a writer
since you gave up acting, not that you've made much effort to
write since your first two plays were turned down.

ROBERT. I see. So really you're only using your knowledge of
my little peccadilloes as a way of threading together my life as
a failure.

ANNE. You are a failure. You're not even what you used to call yourself, a success manqué. You're a failure.

ROBERT. Thank you. Thank you, darling.

ANNE. I'm sorry. But he said that when I was ready to tell you, I mustn't try to spare your feelings.

ROBERT. He did, did he? I see.

ANNE. Haven't you wondered what I was really doing, all those afternoons these last six months.

ROBERT. You said you had director's notes, publicity, interviews, lunches with — no, I haven't. I haven't wondered. Who is it? What's his name?

ANNE. Widdecombe.

ROBERT. I don't know any Widdecombe, he's not an actor.

ANNE. Of course he isn't. He's an analyst.

ROBERT. An analyst? An analyst of what?

ANNE. People. People like me. And you.

ROBERT. You mean he's a shrink! You've been having an affair with a shrink!

ANNE. I haven't been having an affair with him. I've been seeing him professionally. I was desperate, you see, quite desperate without knowing why, all I knew was that I didn't want to talk to you about it, which was significant in itself, and all the good things that had happened, my third West End success in a row, the Evening Standard Best Actress, the Plays and Players Best Actress — didn't seem to matter a damn, and then I remembered that supper we had with Humphry Ditch last year, and he told us about the analyst who'd sorted him out when he'd had a near break-down over that revolting little Tunisian boy —

ROBERT. May I remind you that Glycerine Ditch committed suicide two months ago. Or is that your Widdecombe's idea of sorting people out.

ANNE. That was over the antiques swindle he got caught out in — he was going to go to jail —

ROBERT. Anne — Anne darling — for God's sakes — look, all right, I admit, I admit perhaps I've been a bit naughty over those girls — and perhaps I haven't tried enough to — get my own career going again — but Christ, you didn't need to go to a shrink to find that out —

ANNE. That's not what I found out. I knew all that. What I needed was Widdecombe to help me get a perspective —

ROBERT. Just a minute — I'm just beginning to realise — you lay there on his couch and told him — told him all about us, about me and — and you talk of *my* infidelities — oh, I bet he had a wonderful time nodding and clucking the famous Anne O'Neill through her marital problems —

ANNE. As a matter of fact he doesn't know who I am. I gave him an assumed name.

ROBERT. What?

ANNE. Ellen Winterspot.

ROBERT. Ellen Winterspot.

ANNE. I made it up, because that's what I felt like. Hell in Winter spot. And I wore one of my wigs and dark glasses — he knew I was in disguise, and he approved — he says that people in masks are more likely to tell the truth. Especially women. Actually I doubt if he'd know who I was anyway, he seems to have no interest in the theatre or television or anything like that, he's mostly interested in money. In fact he's a bit like a bookie. But I'm deeply grateful to him. I've come to think of him as the sanest and wisest man I've ever met. (*She takes a card out of her pocket.*) Here's his card.

ROBERT. Thank you. Are you doing some part time as his sales rep.?

ANNE. I think you should see him. He says from what he's heard about you you need help far more than I do. He says my only real problem was you — not recognising what a sterile marriage of accommodation and sexless comfort I'd betrayed myself into.

ROBERT. Sexless! What does he mean, sexless!

ANNE. We haven't fucked for months.

ROBERT. You've been too tired.

ANNE. Last night when you came to bed, all buttoned up in your nice new silk pyjamas, grumbling because the battery had run out on your tooth-brush, and in those floppy carpet-slippers — all on my account from Harrods — and climbed between the sheets with a little noise somewhere between a grunt and a purr, you reminded me of that theatre critic, the one you called the Spayed Cat. I described that to Widdecombe this afternoon. He said actually your self-pampering, your domesticity, your perpetual promiscuity and the insult all these things are to me, in my womanhood, aren't just symptoms of your failure, but of something deeper wrong with you. He thinks you're probably a repressed homosexual. And then I remembered that when I first met you I thought you were gay. Widdecombe says first sexual impressions are usually right.

ROBERT. I can't believe — I don't believe — that you can believe —

ANNE. Widdecombe says you've got to go.

ROBERT. Widdecombe — *Widdecombe* says — (*Laughs.*)

ANNE. He's right. I want you gone, Robert, and I won't have you making any trouble or fuss about it. I'm far more ruthless than you, we've both always known that, and I'll do anything, however cruel, to get you out of my life.

ROBERT. This isn't true — this isn't happening — I'm not some bloody servant or gigolo —

ANNE. Yes you are. That's exactly what you are. Widdecombe used both those words of you. But I don't need a servant or gigolo anymore, I didn't make you into one in the first place. You did it yourself. You're going Robert.

ROBERT. Oh no I'm not, Anne. Oh no I'm not. I'm not going. not anywhere. This is my home. I love it. I've spent years — seven years — nursing you and your monstrous ego from one crisis to another, one triumph to another, I've listened to you night after night after night whine and snivel and bitch, I've

fed you, I've comforted you, I've kept you calm when you
were frightened and together when you were going to pieces,
that's seven years *hard*, Anne, seven years hard with a vain,
boring not particularly talented and totally selfish woman,
i.e. an actress, and all I've got to show for it are a few badly
needed luxuries and hard-earned comforts, and this home,
which is mine, not yours, mine, because I've loved it and
looked after it and appointed it and put up with you in it
for its sake, and I'm not leaving it, Christ I'm not leaving it,
on the say-so of your Widdecombe. I'll kill him first.

ANNE. Widdecombe suggests that a five thousand pound cash
settlement for the work you've done to the house, and for
your sexual, emotional and domestic services over the years,
would be quite adequate. He's had a great deal of
experience in these matters. Anyway, it should tide you over
and into your new life. If I were you, I'd think about going
back into stage-management, it really is your forte, and I've
kept up payments on your Equity card, haven't I? You can
take all personal gifts from me, and all the gifts you've
given yourself from me, including the portable but not the
electric type-writer. No furniture and only your own books.

ROBERT. There aren't any books here, except the ones I've
bought. You don't read anything unless it's got your
photograph in the middle of it — Anne O'Neill, a very
private person, and her husband Robert Simon, out of
camera —

ANNE. You have until Wednesday afternoon to clear out. I shall
come back promptly at four, with your cheque in my hand,
and if you're still here at five minutes past I shall tear it up and
call the police to have you removed. Until then I'm staying in
London. Don't attempt to see me, and don't you come
anywhere near the theatre and ruin my performance. Or no
cheque and I'll fight you for every stitch of clothing you
haven't paid for, which means everything including the
knickers you're standing up in. (*She goes to the door, left.*)
If I were you, I'd spend some of the five thousand on
Widdecombe. If he'll accept you. He's very choosey as well as
expensive.

ROBERT. Have you any idea what you're just done?

ANNE. I've tossed you out. And it's been just what Widdecombe said it would be. The most exhilarating act of my life. If you do decide to see him, you can tell him who Ellen Winterspot was and that he was right, I'm cured, and give him my greetings and my thanks. Now I'll just go and get some clothes and night things, and I'll leave. (*She goes out through the kitchen.*)

ROBERT *stands, stunned. He goes to the side-board, pours himself a glass of wine. Doesn't drink it. Takes out a bottle of scotch. Pours himself a glass of that. Begins to walk up and down, drinking. Suddenly stops, looks at the card in his hand.*

ROBERT. Ha! (*He walks.*) Ha! (*Makes as if to hurl his glass through the french windows.*)

HERMAN (*enters through them*). Oh, you've finished your supper then?

ROBERT *lowers the glass.*

HERMAN. How was the pheasant, nice?

ROBERT. Ashes, ashes, as ashes.

HERMAN. Oh, yes. I can smell burning.

ROBERT. My soul.

HERMAN. What?

ROBERT. What do you want, Herman?

HERMAN. Is Anne safely out of the way?

ROBERT. Quite safely.

HERMAN. Then here. Take this. (*He hands him the gun, from his pocket.*)

ROBERT (*takes it*). Why?

HERMAN. And this. (*He takes out of his pocket, an extremely large flick knife, the blade in. He presses it out as he shows it to ROBERT.*)

ROBERT *starts back, reflexively.*

HERMAN. Another symbol! See. (*He flicks it back in.*) She was gone by the time I got there, but this was lying on my pillow. Take it! Go on! (*He presses it into* ROBERT's *hand.*) I don't know what she means, whether to kill her, or to kill her husband or to kill myself even, but I can't keep my eyes off them, Robert, or my hands, I've been sitting in the cottage with one in one hand and one in the other and they frighten me, what I could do with them, I'm beginning to think I'm in the middle of a nightmare, so if you'd keep them here somewhere out of my way I'd be ever so grateful. And somewhere where Anne won't see them, of course. The truth is, I've even imagined myself using them on him. (*Pause.*) See what I mean, Robert?

ROBERT. Yes.

HERMAN. Right. Thanks Robert. Thanks. Now I'm going to go and write her a letter care of the London Symphony Orchestra.

ROBERT. Will it get to her there?

HERMAN. Oh yes. It'll get to her all right. She plays the violin for them, you see. She fiddles. She fiddles while I burn, eh? 'Night Robert. And give my goodnights to Anne. (*He goes out through the french windows.*)

ROBERT *stands holding the knife closed in one hand, the pistol in the other.*

ANNE (*enters through the kitchen, carrying some clothes over her arm, a sponge-bag, etc*). Four o'clock. Wednesday. (*Makes towards the door, left.*)

ROBERT. Just a minute darling. (*Shows her the gun, the knife.*) I've got some goodnights to give you.

ANNE *stares at him. As he takes a step towards her, he releases the blade; she screams. On her scream:*

Lights

Scene Two

Several days later. Robert descends from the loft, drawing a rope down from the flap. Brushes his hands, then goes to the door, takes a key out of his pocket, tests the lock, leaves the key in, goes to the desk, picks up the revolver, puts it in his pocket, as the sound is heard of a car arriving, off left. ROBERT looks towards left, glances around as if checking, then goes over and draws the curtains over the french windows. There is a ring on the door-bell, left.

> ROBERT *goes off, left. There is the sound of a door opening, off left.* WIDDECOMBE *enters.* ROBERT *follows, closes the door, locks it deftly, slides the key into his pocket, as* WIDDECOMBE *turns.*

ROBERT. Well, here you are, then?

WIDDECOMBE. Yes.

ROBERT. And on time, too. So no mishaps. I mean, you weren't mugged by West Indians, or bombed by Irishmen, or ganged up on by squads of Japanese in dark suits or sang at by Welshmen or bought up by an Arab. Oh, I must be careful, or you'll think I'm xenophobic too, and that's really not one of my problems. A Xenophobe in England today would be in an even worse pickle than I am, I should think? (*Laughs.*) I'm trying to make chit-chat, probably not the right thing to do, as it seems to be coming out all wrong. Look, you say something.

WIDDECOMBE. It's rather dark in here, isn't it?

ROBERT. Yes I know, but so cosy and snug. Do you mind? I thought you chaps were used to working in it. Burrowing down and down so to speak, through the layers of phoney brightness.

WIDDECOMBE. But we like to see the people we're dealing with, if we can.

ROBERT. Right. Right. Well — um, well, I'll tell you what, I'll put them on, but I won't open the curtains if you don't mind — I don't like glimpses into the wings, if you see, it always looks so unreal out there — (*Turning on the lights*) — there —

and there — and there — (*The room is now hideously over-lit.*)
How's that?

WIDDECOMBE (*blinking*). Well, a trifle bright perhaps.

ROBERT. Still, I'm glad you suggested it. Now I can see you in
detail, you look jolly comforting.

WIDDECOMBE. Good. But will you allow me — (*He turns off a
couple of lights.*)

ROBERT. How's that?

WIDDECOMBE. Just right.

ROBERT. I'm so glad. Can I get you anything else before we
begin?

WIDDECOMBE. No thank you.

ROBERT. Well — perhaps later you'll think of something?

WIDDECOMBE. Yes, perhaps later.

ROBERT. If you do, you will mention it?

WIDDECOMBE. I will.

ROBERT. Right. What sort of thing do you think it's likely to
be?

WIDDECOMBE. Well, I won't know that until I've thought of it.

ROBERT. No, of course you won't. Just like God himself, eh?

WIDDECOMBE. Like God?

ROBERT. Well, nothing exists unless he thinks of it. Which is
why he has to keep thinking about himself. To go on existing.
Which doesn't give him much time to think properly about the
rest of us. Which is why we all lead such half and half and
finally temporary existences. What do you think of that, or is
it all a bit too theoretical for you?

WIDDECOMBE. It is rather.

ROBERT. Oh, I'm glad you're going to take a practical and down-
to-earth tone — I can't tell you how grateful I am to you. For
coming here like this. The way you responded to my midnight
S.O.S. was very moving.

WIDDECOMBE. You're obviously in great trouble.

ROBERT. I am, I am, but I've made lots of troubled 'phone calls over the years, to plumbers and gas-men when our boiler's gone and so forth, they could take a leaf out of your book, I can tell you — not that they'd make much of it, they can scarecely understand the instructions in their own manuals, we had one just the other day, the sweetest little Pakistani — oh, I'm off again, and I'm so anxious to get started, shall I just take the plunge, I've got a couch ready, go to it and lie on it and surrender myself to you. Like they do in all those cartoons and films and plays — shall I? (*Going to the couch.*)

WIDDECOMBE. Well, first there are a couple of little matters I'd like to get straightened out. I would have explained on the 'phone but you hung up so quickly —

ROBERT. I know, I'm so sorry. But I was frightened you'd change your mind, and I've heard such things about you — the effect you have on people, how you go to the very heart with your capacious and incisive intelligence — a force, a force for life as it were — and I didn't want to lose you by chatter-boxing on as I am now. And give myself away with some significant slip — I mean I didn't want you pegging me as a ghastly little pansy before you'd even clapped eyes on me. Oh — (*Claps his hand to his mouth.*) Oh that's all right, isn't it, they won't get me for that will they.

WIDDECOMBE. Who?

ROBERT. Those language purists we hear so much about these days. But as long as I work on the reverse principle, I'm a pansy, you're queer, but he's gay. And so is she. If you follow. Then that's safe, isn't it?

WIDDECOMBE. Perhaps we can follow that up in a minute. But — now can we just —

ROBERT. What? Oh yes. I'm sorry. So sorry. Those things I didn't give you the chance — what are they?

WIDDECOMBE. Well firstly, this can only be an exploratory session. I can't commit myself further at this stage.

ROBERT. Commit yourself?

WIDDECOMBE. To accepting you as a patient.

ROBERT. Accepting me? I see. So really you're the sort of Garrick Club of the mentally distressed? Well I hope I get in.

WIDDECOMBE. Secondly, if I do decide that we should go further, you should realise that it's likely to be a long-term business.

ROBERT. How long?

WIDDECOMBE. I've had some people on my books for ten years.

ROBERT. Ten years — well, that only proves how much they must like you. I switch dentists all the time, I can never find one to suit. No no — you haven't said anything to put me off. I'm going to do my best to qualify.

WIDDECOMBE. There's a third thing.

ROBERT. Yes.

WIDDECOMBE. I'm very expensive.

ROBERT. Good God of course you are. You *must* be. I mean you can't just dispense your diagnoses as if they were horoscopes in the evening papers!

WIDDECOMBE. I charge thirty pounds a session.

ROBERT. Oh. (*Little pause.*) Well —

WIDDECOMBE. For a preliminary consultation, which this is, I charge fifty pounds. Plus expenses. The petrol, and a cancelled session with another patient. Would be seventy pounds in all. And I have to ask for it in advance.

ROBERT (*after a pause*). Perfectly fair! because if you don't get it in advance, you might never get it at all. Right? (*He goes to the desk.*) Seventy pounds did you say? (*He takes a cheque out of the drawer, writes.*) What initial?

WIDDECOMBE. F.

ROBERT. F for?

WIDDECOMBE. Just F will do.

ROBERT (*writes, brings the cheque around, hands it to him*). This is part of your therapy isn't it?

WIDDECOMBE. What? (*Taking the cheque.*)

ROBERT. Well, I feel better already. This simple transaction means that I've got you all to myself, doesn't it? And the feeling of confidence that gives me — I have got you all to myself, haven't I? I mean nobody from your office is going to disturb us, nobody knows you're here, do they?

WIDDECOMBE. Only my secretary.

ROBERT. Do you sleep with her?

WIDDECOMBE. It's a him, actually.

ROBERT. Is it? Well, do you sleep with it, then? (*Laughs.*) See. I feel I can take risks with you now. Tease you a little. That must be good, mustn't it? But look, I've just thought of something — Supposing I fall in love with you, that's quite usual isn't it, and then you reject me? Or I fall in love with you and you accept me but I need to see so much of you at thirty pounds a session that I'm impoverished and *then* you reject me — what would become of me then, Widdecombe?

WIDDECOMBE. Let's not worry about that right now. Let's see if we can find out what's the matter with you. Why did you 'phone me?

ROBERT. Well, I — well, the worst thing is this room. You've already noticed — I can't bring myself to leave it — except to perform my natural bodily functions and gulp down a glass of milk and a crust. It's as if it were a — a stage, do you see, and I was going to be forced to play out some hideous drama of murder. Suicide. Revenge.

WIDDECOMBE. So you're suffering from acute agoraphobia.

ROBERT. Is that what it's called. Oh good!

WIDDECOMBE. With traces of psychosis and persecution mania.

ROBERT. Oh good.

WIDDECOMBE. You can get on the sofa now.

ROBERT (*goes over to the sofa, sits on the edge then lies down*). The funny thing is — (*Lying down.*) — that now I'm here, prone, my whole body at your mercy —

WIDDECOMBE *draws up a chair and puts his hand inside his jacket, fiddles briefly.*

ROBERT. I feel a little frightened of you suddenly.

WIDDECOMBE. That's because I'm an authority figure. You need my help, but you resent and fear me. You're married, aren't you?

ROBERT. How do you know?

WIDDECOMBE. Because you've been *acting* queer.

ROBERT. How did you know?

WIDDECOMBE. Because you've been acting it badly.

ROBERT *(coldly)*. I see.

WIDDECOMBE. Which means that you were signalling to me that you weren't. You didn't want me to be taken in, in other words. You're married, aren't you?

ROBERT. Yes.

WIDDECOMBE. Something's gone wrong with the marriage, has it?

ROBERT. Can we talk about it later, please?

WIDDECOMBE. I'd rather talk about it now. Don't worry, nothing you say will shock me.

ROBERT. Still, later please.

WIDDECOMBE. I'll come back to it very soon. It's important. Right, tell me about your father.

ROBERT. Daddy?

WIDDECOMBE. Yes. Daddy.

ROBERT. Well what?

WIDDECOMBE. Begin with your last memory of him.

ROBERT. Well — he was lying on the bed — his and Mummy's — and she was bent over him, doing something to his flies. Buttoning them up, I suppose. She always tended to him on special occasions, you see.

WIDDECOMBE (*suppressing a yawn*). What was the special occasion?

ROBERT. His funeral. Shouldn't you be taking this down — they always do in plays —

WIDDECOMBE. I know how to do my job. What was she like, your mother?

ROBERT. Oh, very much in the usual run of mothers, really. She was — well tall, voluptuous, with warm, inviting eyes.

WIDDECOMBE. Dead too, is she?

ROBERT. Oh no — don't say that — (*Rearing up*) — please Widdecombe!

WIDDECOMBE. You said was. She was.

ROBERT. Yes, *was* tall, voluptuous, so forth, but now she *is* a bit shrunken, her hair's white, what there is of it, and her eyes run. She's in her eighties, we were very close to begin with, but then we grew apart. I was a forceps delivery, do you think that's significant, and another thing, once she caught me playing with myself in my bath, I was only thirteen —

WIDDECOMBE. And now your wife.

ROBERT. You're being very cruel.

WIDDECOMBE. Answer my questions, please. Don't worry if they seem out of sequence or a bit eccentric, I know what I'm doing. How often have you been unfaithful to her?

ROBERT. What?

WIDDECOMBE. How often have you been unfaithful to your wife?

ROBERT. Well — (*Little pause.*) — three hundred and fifty seven times, at the last count. But that includes one nights and uprights in cupboards and on the stairs, some of them were really more like finger-jabs — even so you don't seem very impressed.

WIDDECOMBE. Has she been unfaithful to you?

ROBERT. No. But there's a man in her life, Widdecombe, what

you call an authority figure, who's poisoned her against me.

WIDDECOMBE. And do you hate him?

ROBERT. Oh yes. I intend to ruin him.

WIDDECOMBE. And her?

ROBERT. Ah. Ah—hah. (*Little pause.*) What's the time?

WIDDECOMBE. Half three. What do you mean, ah—hah? Have you harboured any desires to kill her? Have you behaved violently towards her?

ROBERT. Yes. (*Laughs.*)

WIDDECOMBE. So to sum up. You've committed three hundred and fifty seven acts of infidelity. As far as you know, your wife isn't sexually unfaithful to you. She's turned for help and advice to an older man. This has made you jealous, you want to hurt her because of it, is that right?

ROBERT. A rather bald outline, surely Widdecombe —

WIDDECOMBE. We won't get anywhere unless you're honest. Is it right?

ROBERT. Yes. You've got an alarming amount of the policeman in you — I feel less inclined to fall in love with you — are you going?

WIDDECOMBE (*has risen*). I've got enough.

ROBERT. Rather a short session, for seventy pounds.

WIDDECOMBE. It's not the length, it's the depth.

ROBERT. And when will I see you again.

WIDDECOMBE. You won't be seeing me again, Mr. Simon. If you're sensible.

ROBERT. You don't want my money, then?

WIDDECOMBE. You haven't got enough, is my impression. Whatever money there is, isn't yours, it's your wife's, is my impression.

ROBERT. Indeed. And what gives you that impression?

WIDDECOMBE. The way you throw it around. She's either left

you or leaving you, isn't she?

ROBERT. No, she's not. In fact, she's coming straight down. You can see her for yourself. (*He strides to the rope, pulls it.*) Darling — you're on!

The trap door to the loft opens. ANNE's *body, with a rope around its neck, arms and feet tied, tongue protruding, eyes bulging, comes plummetting down.* HERMAN's *knife is plunged into her chest. There are blood-stains around it.*

ROBERT. Her greetings — and her thanks, Widdecombe! (*He laughs insanely.*)

Lights.

Curtain

ACT TWO

As before. Two seconds later. The body is still twitching.

ROBERT. All right, I concede it's not one of the great coups, but in Worthing it made a small boy actually sick with terror. Right over the hat of the woman in front of him . . Of course they tried to take that away from me too by claiming it was the hat that did it. (*He takes the knife out as he talks.*)

WIDDECOMBE (*is studying the mask*). Is this meant to be your wife?

ROBERT. Well, of course I've never seen her with quite that expression. Except when reading some of her reviews. You're a coolish customer, Widdecombe, I'll give you that. I've been responsible for some flops in my time —

WIDDECOMBE. But her hair's like this, is it?

ROBERT. Isn't it? (*Stands, facing Widdecombe, knife pointing towards him.*)

WIDDECOMBE (*after a pause*). Will you put that down, please.

ROBERT. Why?

WIDDECOMBE. I don't like knives.

ROBERT. Oh. (*Little pause.*) Sorry. (*He puts the knife down.*) Well, I still haven't aroused your interest in my situation?

WIDDECOMBE. What's interesting about a trick like that?

ROBERT. Well, what about my agoraphobia, my being imprisoned in this room?

WIDDECOMBE. There's the door. Go through it.

ROBERT. But how?

WIDDECOMBE. That's your problem, old man. (*He turns, goes to the door left.*)

ROBERT *watches him, smiling.* WIDDECOMBE *tries the door, several times.*

ROBERT. It seems to be your problem, too.

WIDDECOMBE (*comes back*). Key please.

ROBERT *smiles.*

WIDDECOMBE. I don't like being locked in rooms I want to get out of.

ROBERT. You like your freedom, do you?

WIDDECOMBE. Give me the key.

ROBERT. But a very limited freedom, if it means you have to exit through the door you entered by. There are doors behind the curtains, you know. They're open.

WIDDECOMBE *looks towards the curtains. Goes to them.*

ROBERT (*takes the pistol out of his pocket*). Oh Widde-combe — (*In a singing voice. Points the gun at him.*) Moment please. Old cheese. Something you haven't realised.

WIDDECOMBE *stops, turns, stares at* ROBERT. ROBERT *walks slowly towards him, pointing the gun at his stomach.*

Of course, freedom is also a matter of having the nerve to exit through doors you haven't entered by, when doing so may bring a bullet in the back. Or gut. On the other hand it may bring fresh air, the scent of roses, a sunny path to a gate in an ivied wall, a stroll around the house to your car — freedom, in other words, is an indifference to consequences. That was rehearsed, I'm afraid. This moment means too much to me to be improvised. Which do you choose, Widdecombe? (*Little pause.*) Do you need a prompt? (*Turns, fires into the dummy, which jumps.*) See. It is.

WIDDECOMBE. I'll stay.

ROBERT. Thank you. Come right back then, if you please.

WIDDECOMBE (*comes back into the room*). If you want your money back, I'll be only too happy —

ROBERT. No no. I'm sure you'll earn it in the end. Would you strike that prop though, please.

WIDDECOMBE. What?

ROBERT. Sorry. The jargon of my ex-trade. As 'authority figure' is of yours. So 'strike the prop authority figure' translates as 'get rid of the dummy, shrink'. (*Little pause.*) Just pull on the rope.

> WIDDECOMBE *pulls on the rope. The dummy goes back into the loft.*

ROBERT. Thank you. Anything like this ever happened to you before, Widders?

WIDDECOMBE. No.

ROBERT. What, no violent patients, ever?

WIDDECOMBE. Well, not with me.

ROBERT (*with concern*). But you're trembling.

WIDDECOMBE. Yes. I don't like guns you see.

ROBERT. I say, you are a chap with pronounced dislikes. You don't like knives, don't like being locked in rooms, don't like discarded gigolos, don't like guns — and yet here you are, locked in a room by a discarded gigolo who's got a gun and a knife and doesn't like you. And I'm afraid the fact that you've chosen to exercise your freedom by coming back into the room because I threatened to shoot you, doesn't mean I can't exercise mine by shooting you anyway, does it? (*He points the gun into* WIDDECOMBE's *face.*)

> WIDDECOMBE *says something.*

ROBERT. Now Widdecombe. No asides, please.

WIDDECOMBE. I said don't. Please.

ROBERT. Well, I've certainly bouleversé'd you a little this time, eh? I'm sure you're going to be worth my seventy quid. Let's start a new session. But this time you do the work. Sit down. WIDDECOMBE *goes to sit down.* No, not there. The sight-lines are terrible. Nor there — (*As* WIDDECOMBE *moves to another chair.*) — you'd be up-staging me. Now bring that chair over — that's right! And put it there. I could make a good props man out of you, Widdecombe, if I didn't need you for a leading part. Right. Off you go.

WIDDECOMBE (*after a pause*). What do you want?

ROBERT. A bit of rapid depth analysis. Tell me about yourself.

WIDDECOMBE. Well — um — what?

ROBERT. F. What does it stand for?

WIDDECOMBE. Ferdinand.

ROBERT. I prefer you as Widdecombe. I've got used to you as Widdecombe. Widdecombe calm, Widdecombe threatening, Widdecombe greedy — above all Widdecombe greedy — and now Widdecombe cowed. But all of them Widdecombe. Are you married, Ferdinand?

WIDDECOMBE. Yes.

ROBERT. What's she like, your wife?

WIDDECOMBE. Well — her name's Rosalind.

ROBERT. Oh come, you can do better than that? Is she an anal retentive, a womb hysteric, a penis envier — give us depth, Widdecombe, depth.

WIDDECOMBE. She's — she's very nice. I mean, she's small and — and a bit plump and — and looks after me and the two boys. And — and really — there's nothing wrong with her, you see. She's just — normal. Really.

ROBERT. Do you love her?

WIDDECOMBE. Yes

ROBERT. Is she good in bed?

WIDDECOMBE (*after a little pause*). Yes.

ROBERT. Details.

WIDDECOMB. Well I — she — we have just an ordinary sex life.

ROBERT. You don't want to talk about it?

WIDDECOMBE. No — well, it's difficult —

ROBERT. Right. We'll come back to her in a minute. I expect it's the phallic symbol I'm pointing at your head, distracting, eh?

WIDDECOMBE. Yes.

ROBERT. Now the two boys.

WIDDECOMBE. Well, Piers is ten and Nigel's twelve. Piers is good at football and Nigel — um — well, he stammers. Piers is well-built and Nigel's a bit on the plump side.

ROBERT. Takes after his dad, eh? What about sibling rivalry, masturbation problems, penis envy?

WIDDECOMBE. Just — just the normal amount. No problems really.

ROBERT. What about your father?

WIDDECOMBE. He died when I was six.

ROBERT. Mother?

WIDDECOMBE. She's dead too, last year.

ROBERT. What about your accent? Just ten minutes ago it had a certain plummy confidence, now it's slipping past the suburbs.

WIDDECOMBE. Because — because I'm frightened, I expect.

ROBERT. So it's returning to base, is it?

WIDDECOMBE. Yes.

ROBERT. Tell me about your vices. Be frank but not fearless.

WIDDECOMBE. Well I — I eat too much, and sometimes I have a spot too much to drink.

ROBERT. Go on.

WIDDECOMBE. Well — I go after money a bit too much —

ROBERT That's a symptom of anal retentiveness, isn't it?

WIDDECOMBE. I suppose so. Yes.

ROBERT. Give me a brief résumé of your qualifications and experiences.

WIDDECOMBE. I — I haven't got any.

ROBERT. None at all?

WIDDECOMBE. No, I'm what's called a lay analyst. I don't need any qualifications.

ROBERT. But you must have undergone analysis yourself?

WIDDECOMBE (*after a little pause*). Well, a short period once.

ROBERT. Where, Geneva?

WIDDECOMBE. No, in South Africa.

ROBERT. And what happened?

WIDDECOMBE. They invited me to join the police.

ROBERT. To assist in interrogations?

WIDDECOMBE. That sort of thing.

ROBERT. But you turned them down?

WIDDECOMBE. Yes. The pay wasn't very good — besides Rose — Rosalind didn't want the babies brought up away from her mum — mother.

ROBERT (*Looks at him, shakes his head*). Well, here's my diagnosis. You're a family-loving orphan with swinish appetites and unusual acquisitiveness in a fraudulent profession. But what's beginning to worry me, old bean, is whether you're up to the role I've cast you in. You're such a coarse and palpable fraud, even by the standards of your profession. How do you get away with it? How do you take them in?

WIDDECOMBE. I think it's my manner. They — they like it. They find it very reassuring — I mean, most of the people I get don't know what to do so I tell them.

ROBERT. And they're mostly women, are they?

WIDDECOMBE. Yes. And artists and actors and university teachers. That type. But I've done good — honest.

ROBERT. Guv.

WIDDECOMBE. Pardon?

ROBERT. Shouldn't it be 'honest Guv'.

WIDDECOMBE. I have done good.

ROBERT. All right. Persuade me. One case. Choose carefully. Think quickly. (*Looking at his watch.*) Time's getting on.

WIDDECOMBE. Well, one that comes to mind, an opera singer. She was — she was terrified her voice was going. And it was. From what the papers said. She refused to go on stage three times running, she'd been to all sorts before she came to me — Freudians, Laingians, Jungians — on drugs, drink, I got her functioning again.

ROBERT. Kept her singing?

WIDDECOMBE. Yes — yes, she's still performing, I think. I don't go to the opera myself —

ROBERT. And that's one of your triumphs?

WIDDECOMBE. Yes. Well —

ROBERT. Not good enough, Widdecombe. You've forgotten Bernard Levin.

WIDDECOMBE. Who?

ROBERT. A famous opera lover. He expects the best and he's entitled to the best and he even pays for the best — he may get his tickets free from the management, but his opera-going kit must cost him a fortune, Widdecombe — his cloaks and waist-coats and shiny little pumps, all his fol-de-rol and furbelow — and even if he gets those free from the management too, you still have no right to ruin his evening by putting onto the stage a clapped-out singer who's lost her voice — oh, I take a very serious view of that, Widdecombe. (*Putting the pistol close to* WIDDECOMBE's *head.*)

WIDDECOMBE. Wait! Well there was — there was a — (*Desperately.*)

ROBERT. What?

WIDDECOMBE. Well, there was a lad who came to me because one night he'd blinded some horses, though he loved them, and I made him relive it all again, you see, and I taught him to realise that these horses were really just naked men prancing about in his head —

ROBERT. Widdecombe, Widdecombe, they asked me if I'd be interested in stage-managing that one.

WIDDECOMBE. I'm sorry — it's just that I can't think — think
   like this — all I know is — that I've done some people a lot of
   good, helped them out in their marriages, particularly, got to
   the bottom of things, worked them through their divorces —

ROBERT. Like a private detective.

WIDDECOMBE. Yes. No — I've *helped* people —

ROBERT. Like Ellen Winterspot.

WIDDECOMBE. Who?

ROBERT. You don't remember her?

WIDDECOMBE. Well, I get so many — I can't remember every
   one — not without going through my books.

ROBERT. You know I've been looking forward to this particular
   moment, it was one of the climaxes you see — and I'd worked
   on the speech a little — and now I see what you are, you really
   are — (*Shakes his head*) — still, perhaps I'll get myself going
   eh?

WIDDECOMBE. What?

ROBERT. Ellen Winterspot came to you in a state of stress, of
   course she did, she's always in a state of stress, being highly
   ambitious, extremely vain and hopelessly insecure in a business
   run on ambition, vanity and insecurity, there was nothing out
   of the normally horrendous wrong with her at all, but you
   didn't bother to find that out, did you, you couldn't even be
   bothered to penetrate a simple disguise to find out who she
   really was and what business she was in, you simply gave her
   some of your off-the-cuff advice in your usual brutal style for
   your usual brutal fees, no doubt, months on months of session
   on session of thirty guinea fees, and her marriage, my marriage,
   her happiness, *my home* meant nothing to you at all — you didn't
   give any of it as much as a thought, how could you, clearly
   incapable as you are of giving a thought to anything but the
   profits from your sordid swindles — even with a gun pointing
   at your head — but there were lives at stake, Widdecombe,
   yours among them as it's turned out, because Widdecombe,
   the truth about you is — (*All this with mounting fury.
   Suddenly stops.*) It's no good. Nothing there. Nothing there at

all. You really are a dreadful disappointment, you know. I'd really imagined — ah well, the only thing is to plough on. Get up Widdescombe, the spayed cat is about to strike back. God, what a waste — the spayed cat is about to strike — ah.

WIDDECOMBE. What?

ROBERT. Get up. It's all built around my shooting you, you see. I'll tell you what, I'll give you a last chance — see if you can come up with something — but no clichés or whinings or bang!

WIDDECOMBE. Look, please, please —

ROBERT. That's a whine, Widdecombe.

WIDDECOMBE. I've got a wife. A wife and two kids —

ROBERT. That's a cliché *and* a whine. I can't waste any further time giving you chances. If you can't take the centre, even at a moment like this, you can't. One —

WIDDECOMBE. No — no no —

ROBERT. Two.

WIDDECOMBE. No no no no no —

ROBERT. Three.

WIDDECOMBE. Oh God!

They stare at each other for a second. ROBERT *shoots him in the stomach.* WIDDECOMBE *screams, lurches back, clutching at stomach, stops.*

ROBERT. That last bit was rather good. No notes at all there.

WIDDECOMBE *collapses into a chair.* ROBERT *tosses the gun into* WIDDECOMBE's *lap.*

You're still grasping the first stage of my plan, are you? (*He crosses to the telephone, talks as he dials.*) It's to give you, you see, a vivid taste of death. A glimpse over the abyss. A spasm of eternity. And so forth. So that you'd learn something about the irrationality of the human psyche, those you tamper with so callously — as well as your own. But now please pull yourself together, your next scene is far bigger. Not a simple matter of dying, you know. (*He turns irritably to the telephone.*) Oh, where the Hell are they — come *on* — (*He looks at his watch.*)

WIDDECOMBE (*stands up, still trembling, clearly not aware of what he is saying*). Think you had to teach me — think I don't know — don't see things before I go to sleep just like everybody else, myself laid flat on a board, eyes closed or open staring, and the cheeks funny, and my feet sometimes crossed and sometimes pointed sideways and my arms down along my sides or hands folded across my chest, I got a wife, a wife and two kids, a home in Cricklewood, a small garden, one of my kids has got a stammer and the other's good at football, he despises me, I see it in his eyes when we knock it about in the garden and the old ticker goes tick-tock tick-tock and my head swimming and I stumble about chortling like I was one of them, and when I tell Rosie, I say I've seen it, Rosie, how he despises me, she does her best to comfort and control me, she says of course he doesn't he loves you Fred, we all do, and there I am, I love him and I can't stand Nigel, I want to take him by the throat every time he tries to say butter, *he* loves me all right, but Piers — and Rosie says I smell and sweat and snore at night, and I think yes, well, that's what I am, that's my being to this one and the other one, and what am I doing here, how did it happen, I had a life to lead too, once, what's gone wrong, *what's gone wrong,* it's not fair Fred, this isn't what you had twenty years ago when you were free in Cyprus, a seedy man in a seedy job, and boards and crossed hands and my cheeks, these cheeks funny, why that's not what my Mum meant when she started me out, is it, was it in my Dad's mind when he took her and fired me up her, this is no life for you old man. See. There's nothing you can teach me about anything of that, see, I have the experience all the time, every night, but what you did just now when you fired that at me and made me think and feel is you've made me hate you as I've never hated anyone before, there was a boy called Roger used to wait for me when I went to school, mornings when I went there, evenings coming back, and the things he'd do to me, I thought I'd never hate again as I hated him, but I hate you more, more than Roger Speke, for the way you treated me a minute ago,

I wouldn't have done that, never have done that, to any living person, and let them live through it. (*He stands, still shaking.*)

ROBERT. There, you see. The same thing happened to Dostoievsky, and it had the same sort of effect — perhaps you'll start turning out novels too — what *is* the matter with them, do you think they're on strike — oh, hello Kent Television, News Desk, please. Oh, Kent News, I expect you'd like to hear of the murder of Dr. Robert Simon, *homme de théâtre* — man of the theatre! — of Globe House, Maddingley, Kent. The two parties responsible for his death are Mr. Ferdinand, alias Fred Widdecombe, the distinguished psychoanalyst, and Mr. Simon's wife, Anne O'Neill, that's right, *the* Anne O'Neill, alias Ellen Winterspot — have you got that? So you just toddle along with your cameras etc. and catch Robert Simon's last death appearance — and try to get his face, this time, eh? (*Hangs up.*)

WIDDECOMBE. What? (*He makes towards the french windows.*)

ROBERT (*shoots out the blade of* HERMAN's *knife*). No, no, not yet — (*He points it at* WIDDECOMBE. *Dials again.*) Of course as far as your professional association goes, murdering one of your patients may simply be the ultimate therapy, but the media will take a vivid interest — they'll probably fly Frosty over to conduct the interrogation — and old Anne won't be making it to any Evening Standard Award Luncheons for a while — they're very choosey — good God, they're as bad as — hello, the police! I want to report a murder, the murder of Mr. Robert Simon of Globe House, Maddingley, Kent, by Mr. Ferdinand Widdecombe, Widdecombe and Mrs. Anne Roberts, the deceased's wife. (*Little pause.*) This is the deceased speaking, but it's not a joke, try and make it by a few minutes past four, won't you, the T.V. boys are already on their way, it would look better from your point of view if you managed to get here a few seconds before them (*He hangs up.*) There! See!

WIDDECOMBE. You know what your trouble is. You're mad! (*He makes another attempt to leave.*)

ROBERT. Oh, you're not leaving the stage yet, Widdecombe.

En garde! (*He flashes the knife about, stops.*) Oh, I forgot to tell you — (*as* WIDDECOMBE *cowers back*) — the next bullet in that gun is live. The question is whether you've got the nerve to fire it — I don't think you have, in which case it'll be *your* body that will get the coverage — *en garde!* (*Stops.*) Pick it up, I should.

WIDDECOMBE (*runs to the pistol, picks it up*). Live!

ROBERT. That's right, but you'll never squeeze the trigger — *en garde!* (*Comes flashing towards* **WIDDECOMBE**.)

WIDDECOMBE. Won't I, oh won't I? (*Stands pointing the gun at* ROBERT.) Well, don't try me. After what you did, you're just a walking shit-house, a piss-pot on legs as far as I'm concerned I'll kill, don't you worry.

ROBERT. No, you won't.

WIDDECOMBE. Listen matey, I was in the army out in Cyprus. I did things then would give you nightmares to hear about —

ROBERT (*slashes forward*). You're lying, Widdecombe.

WIDDECOMBE. Oh, am I?Once we caught them once in their truck, made them kneel with their hands on their knees, put a bullet in the back of their heads, then put bullets in them everywhere, the front, their legs, their arms, their bums, then blew the truck up with their own bomb, made a mistake there, it was a big one, Sergeant Winters lost a foot, Hadley had his teeth scattered — I'm telling you this so you'll know. I've had a gun in my hand before, I've killed, I've seen friends die —

ROBERT *jumps forward with the knife.*

WIDDECOMBE (*shrilly, jumping back*). Don't! It's my death I'm afraid of matey, not yours.

ROBERT (*glances at his watch*). Four o'clock. Come on then, Widdecombe — let's see you do it! (*He leaps after him, flashing the knife.*)

WIDDECOMBE (*backing faster and faster*). Don't — don't I tell you — please —

ROBERT *stops, stares at* WIDDECOMBE. WIDDECOMBE

stares back, as if hypnotised. ROBERT *makes a little jump.* WIDDECOMBE *fires.* ROBERT *stops.*

WIDDECOMBE. You — you bastard!

ROBERT. Must be the next one. Try again. (*Pause, then jumps screaming at* WIDDECOMBE.)

WIDDECOMBE *fires.* ROBERT *jerks to a stop, his hand presses to his stomach. Then he lurches towards* WIDDECOMBE, *the knife raised.*

WIDDECOMBE (*retreats behind the sofa*). Don't!

ROBERT (*lurches after him*). Now your turn, WIDDECOMBE! (*He raises the knife.*)

WIDDECOMBE *trapped behind the sofa, shoots again.* ROBERT *spins around, drops the knife, clutches the back of the sofa with one hand.* WIDDECOMBE *squeezes out, steps away.*

ROBERT (*facing the stage, smiles*). Bravo — bravo Widdecombe! (*Blinks for a second, opens his mouth. Blood pours from it. Takes his hand away from his shirt. Blood seeps down from his stomach.*)

WIDDECOMBE *stands, horrified, drops the gun.*
There is the sound of ANNE's *car arriving, off, left.*

ROBERT (*looks at his watch*). Just — perfect — timing. For — her — entrance. But — for — me — bring — bring down — the tabs! The tabs! (*He collapses slowly behind the sofa.*)

There is a pause.

HERMAN (*off, left*). No you stay there until I see —

WIDDECOMBE *looks towards the french windows, then runs towards the door, stage left, tries to open it, remembers, lets out a groan.*

HERMAN (*inside the french windows behind the curtain*). Hey, Robert, you in there, what's going on? (*Pause.*) Mind if I come in. (*Pause. Pulls back the curtains, enters.*) Oh — hi.

WIDDECOMBE. Hello.

There is a pause.

HERMAN. What's going on?

WIDDECOMBE. Pardon?

HERMAN. I heard gun-shots. I heard one earlier, when I was in the cottage.

WIDDECOMBE. Gun back-firing.

HERMAN. A gun?

WIDDECOMBE. Car. I mean. Car back-firing?

HERMAN. That's what I thought the first time, but I was just coming up the road and Robert's wife came by in the car. She let me in to give me a lift and I heard them again. We both did. She's outside, wanting to know what's going on.

WIDDECOMBE. Oh.

HERMAN. It *was* a gun. Where *is* Robert?

WIDDECOMBE. Ah. Not back yet. Waiting for him myself. Actually can't hold on any longer. Tell him I waited, would you. (*He turns to the door, left, stops, when he remembers.*)

HERMAN. Well, who are you?

WIDDECOMBE. Mmmm.

HERMAN. Who *are* you?

WIDDECOMBE. Oh just a chap. (*Pause.*) Looking in. Personal matter. But really can't wait any longer. (*He looks at his watch.*) Good God, nearly four, I'll miss my lunch if I don't hurry. That way's quicker for me. (*He points towards the french windows, then takes a step towards them.*)

HERMAN (*who has been looking around the room*). Christ! A gun! And — and the knife!

WIDDECOMBE. Indeed! (*He makes to pass.*)

HERMAN (*picks the gun up*). You'd better wait a minute, man. Sit down.

WIDDECOMBE *sits down.*

HERMAN. Robert! (HERMAN *takes a few steps towards the*

kitchen, sees behind the sofa. Goes to it, looks down.)

WIDDECOMBE *gets up.*

HERMAN. Je-sus! Jee - sus! He's — he's dead!

WIDDECOMBE. Yes.

HERMAN (*steps away, faces* WIDDECOMBE, *holding the gun*). Sit down, man.

WIDDECOMBE (*sits*). Look — look you see it — it was an accident — he made me do it — he wanted me to do it —

HERMAN. Wanted you to kill him?

WIDDECOMBE. Yes, but it was all a — he thought I was a — because of my being a psychoanalyst.

HERMAN. He wanted you to kill him because he thought you were a psychoanalyst?

WIDDECOMBE. Yes, but I'm not, you see, that's the point. I'm a Private Detective.

HERMAN. You're a Private Detective, is that what you're saying?

WIDDECOMBE. Yes — look let me — listen — (*He puts his hand in his pocket.*)

HERMAN *checks him with the gun.*

WIDDECOMBE. If you'll just — it's my tape-recorder — (*He takes out the tape-recorder carefully.*) Listen. (*He presses a switch.*)

ROBERT (*on tape*). Daddy?

WIDDECOMBE (*on tape*). Yes. Daddy.

ROBERT (*on tape*). Well what?

WIDDECOMBE (*on tape*). Begin with your last clear memory of him.

ROBERT (*on tape*). Well — he was lying on the bed — his and Mummy's — and she was bent over him, doing something to his flies.

WIDDECOMBE (*turning it off*). See.

HERMAN (*takes the tape-recorder from him*). You were trying to get something on Robert's parents?

WIDDECOMBE. No, no, that wasn't a good — no, on him. I've got lots of stuff, boasting about his three hundred and fifty seven girls, wanting to kill his wife, that sort of thing. Masses of stuff. For the divorce, you see. The settlement, all the usual — look, it was his wife's idea — she came to me with a proposition — she wanted shot of him, and she had all the money and he was broke, he's been living off her for years, see, but she said he was the sort to make trouble and screw her for all he could get and she wasn't having it, but she could persuade him to see a shrink, see, she'd set it up that she'd recommend me, and she even had a card printed with my name on it — I've still got them, look — Consultant and all those letters, F. Widdecombe — but here's my real card, see — Private Enquiries, Complete Discretion — Pre-Marital Investigations Our Speciality, Mediterranean Clients Especially Welcome — that's me, what I really am. See.

HERMAN. And you say his wife — his wife — Anne was behind this.

WIDDECOMBE. Well, Mrs. Robert Simon she said her name was — yes, it was all her plan, to get me close, ask questions, she told me how to behave and a few words to use, she said he was so obsessed with himself he wouldn't notice me anyway, thing was to get him chattering ask a few questions about his girls, his wife, that, and get down anything useful, she didn't tell me what he was really like, that he was a real nutter and that he had it in for shrinks, the things he did, a dummy and then shooting me with a blank and then coming at me with a knife and making me kill him all because he hated shrinks, see.

HERMAN. Then why didn't you tell him you were a private detective?

WIDDECOMBE. I thought about it, but then I thought that'd make him even worse — I mean the way I'd tricked him and — and look, I've *got* it, if you don't believe me — 'phone the police, that's right, *he* 'phoned them, see, told them I'd killed him before I had, now I haven't 'phoned, you know that, and you haven't, have you, that'll help me, that'll prove it, you'll be able to tell them it must have been him, go on — go on, 'phone them now and ask them.

HERMAN. You want me to 'phone the police, is that right?

WIDDECOMBE. Yes — yes — please — it's my only chance. Please.

HERMAN (*goes to the telephone, dials*). Has anyone 'phoned in to report the murder of Mr. Robert Simon. That's right, Robert Simon. (*Little pause.*) Oh, well in that case, I'm reporting it now — yes, he's been murdered, shot — Globe House, Maddingley, Kent, yes, right. (*He puts the telephone down, stares at* WIDDECOMBE.)

WIDDECOMBE. Then he — he pretended — I don't understand — but it's all true — true I tell you.

HERMAN. You can't tell me that a lady like Anne would have anything to do with something like this, what a story!

ANNE (*appears nervously at the french windows*). Robert — Herman — what *is* going on.

As she enters, she sees the gun. There is a pause.

HERMAN. You'd better wait outside, Anne,

ANNE. No, I want to know what's going on, where's Robert? (*After a pause.*) Where is he?

HERMAN. The thing is Anne — look — there's been a — it seems as if — as if — there's been an accident.

ANNE. Robert?

HERMAN. He's dead, Anne. But don't look. He's — he's over there. Behind the sofa.

ANNE *goes to sofa.*

HERMAN. No, don't Anne —

ANNE *looks, turns quickly, in horror.*

HERMAN. And this bloke did it. I've sent for the police, but — well I don't know if you can follow this, but perhaps I'd better warn you. This bloke says Robert made him, gave him a gun and then attacked him with a knife to get him to shoot him, and some stuff about pretending to be a psychoanalyst and that — well, Anne, that *you'd* put him up to it.

ANNE (*looks at* WIDDECOMBE). I. He says I — you say I put you up to it?

WIDDECOMBE. That's not her. I've never seen her before — yes, I have, on television, advertising something, baked beans.

ANNE. I happen to be an actress! And I've never seen *you* before in my life.

WIDDECOMBE. No, well you're not the one. She had long blond hair and dumpy and funny teeth.

ANNE. But you killed him.

WIDDECOMBE. He set me up. He set me up. I don't understand the rest of it, but I know that much. (*Gets up.*) Well, I'm going. You won't shoot me — it's hard to pull a trigger on somebody — and even if you do I don't care. I'm going.

HERMAN. They'll catch you. I've got your card.

WIDDECOMBE. Oh, I know that. It happened just as I said, but they won't believe me. Not a chance. I've got a record. Breaking|and entering, a bit of receiving, forging official documents to get my licence — they'll think I shot him when he caught me trying to steal — he can't tell them any different even if he wanted to, can|he, and that woman's not going to come forward now and say she had anything to do with it, is she, whoever she is, so I'm going home, I've got to explain to Rosie and speak to the kids. Prepare them. They've a right — I've got a right — to that. Tell them they can find me at home. Unless you're going to shoot me. Are you?

HERMAN. I can't Anne.

WIDDECOMBE *goes out. There is a pause.*

HERMAN. Jesus Annie! Jesus Christ! It worked.

ANNE. Yes darling, you're as brilliant as you say. I feel rather cold.

HERMAN (*goes over, puts an arm around her*). Now come on Annie, you know me, I'm not some creepy wizard, I'm your simple-minded outgoing Okker boy, don't go getting frightened of me — look, it was just an instinct with someone like Robert, that's all.

ANNE. We got him killed, darling.

HERMAN. No, we didn't Annie. He got *himself* killed. All we did was create a highly charged situation, in which he felt humiliated, rejected and deprived, and then provided him with someone to blame it on, and then gave him a loaded gun and a knife and kept out of the way while he got on with it. That's all we did. Now that may be a bit of a sin, but it's no crime, as my old English teacher used to say — I mean, old Robert could have done any number of things Anne, he could have given me back the gun and knife and left quietly, with his little tail between his legs, the way you asked him to, or he could have played out some fool charade with old Widdecombe, which is what I expected, and left us with the goods on him — Jesus, three hundred and fifty seven, eh Annie, what a monkey! — or he could have killed old Widdecombe and not got killed himself — it was a multi-option situation, Annie, and the options were all his. Now you cling on to that — and that reminds me, I'd better look after this — (*He puts the tape-recorder into his pocket.*)

ANNE. Well, one of the options he nearly took, darling, was to put a bullet in me and carve me up with that ghastly knife!

HERMAN. I know Annie, that was terrible, I thought you'd gone, you see, I looked in and there he was all by himself, and just in the best stage to plonk into his hand something lethal — and then when I left you came back into the room, I was watching through the french windows to see what he'd do next — Jesus! But I wouldn't have let him harm you. Annie, I'd have thought of something, you know that! You're safe with me. (*He hugs her again.*) Now is there anything else besides the tape-recorder — no, there can't be, can there — (*striding about, looking*) — that's the beauty of it, nothing to do with us — just like Brucie, all over again.

ANNE. Brucie.

HERMAN. Didn't I tell you about Brucie, my kid brother, that's where I got the idea from — when he was six and I was eight he used to give me a real wanker's time of it, always telling tales and pinching my cricket pads, so one day I heard Mum telling Dad that she'd caught him playing with the matches again, and that if we didn't look out little Brucie would set himself on fire, which was all right with me, I can tell you, so I took the matches down from the mantle-shelf in the kitchen and stuck them where he'd find them in the toilet after breakfast along with the morning papers and Dad's lighter fluid, and sure enough up he toddled to relieve himself and in no time smoke was pouring out of the toilet window, he's still got the scar-tissue on his bum.

ANNE. Oh.

HERMAN. I know just what you want Annie, you want a Herman special to set you on your feet — eh? And I want an Annie special — (*kissing her*) — and Annie, the way you looked at Widdecombe. Straight in the eye. That was great acting. Hours in his office fixing it up with him to get himself killed or convicted, and he thought he might have seen you selling baked beans!

ANNE. It must have been my Portia, that was my last telly. But I knew he wouldn't recognise me — all he could see was long blond hair, funny teeth and those obsene falsies.

HERMAN. I'll bet you were a great Portia.

ANNE. I didn't wear a blond wig, funny teeth or falsies for Portia.

HERMAN. Well, I'll still bet you were a great Portia. (*He looks at her.*)

ANNE (*suddenly laughs*). You're a swine.

HERMAN. There, that's better — (*He takes her in his arms.*) Oh, I want you — I really could go one right now — to celebrate — tell you the truth, I'm high on it, Annie, but I'd better control myself, don't want the police turning up while we're having it away on the sofa, with hubby lying dead behind it. Eh?

ANNE (*laughs again*). Oh, I mustn't — it's just the thought of him — the only part he could *ever* play — lying dead behind sofas waiting for the police — do you think they'll let me go on tonight, that's what I want to do, that's what I need to do, I'd give the performance of my life —

HERMAN. No Annie, that's out of the question.

ANNE. Yes, they'd say I was hard, wouldn't they — but it is really rather a beautiful part, so fragile, so wistful.

HERMAN. *You* make it fragile and wistful, Annie. (*Going to the telephone.*)

ANNE. I know. But the writer did bring *something* to it — even if I had to change all his lines —

HERMAN (*dialling*). When are we going to get married, Annie, how long will we have to wait?

ANNE. Well (*Little pause.*) I don't know darling.

HERMAN. Of course I can't move in straight away, but then on the other hand I could, as a friend to keep an eye on you after the tragedy — oh hello, is that the police, what's going on in the matter of Mr. Robert Simon's murder, the man who did it's on the run, Mrs. Simon has arrived on the scene and she's a very upset lady — are you on strike, or what? (*Little pause.*) Jesus, well how long then? (*Listens put the 'phone down.*) They're working to rule, Jesus, what a country. But they've left, they'll be here in a few minutes — now how are you going to receive them, Annie, tears or the shakes or should I tuck you up in bed, with a nice cup of tea and do all the talking —

ANNE. Don't worry, darling, I'll improvise quite naturally — one always does find the appropriate response, somehow.

ROBERT *rises up from behind the sofa, shaking, pointing a finger. His eyes upwards, as in death, his mouth open, a great spurt of fresh blood pours from his mouth.* ANNE *screams and screams and screams.*

HERMAN (*gapes*). Jee-sus! (*Terrified*).

ROBERT. Yours — from — the — ranks — of — death! (*He takes a few steps around the sofa.*)

HERMAN *steps back.* ANNE *screams again.* ROBERT *dashes*

over, picks up the gun.

There is a pause.

ROBERT. Sorry. (*He wipes away the blood.*) Couldn't resist using the extra blood capsule. Still, it's what I always say. Certain moments when you *can't* go over the top. (*Little pause.*) You bitch! (*He points the gun at them.*) And as for you, Herman young cheddar, well what a turn-up, eh, thinking you can walk straight out of the bush into the home of an English chappie like me, and take over all his comforts not to mention his wife and her money and their water bed, beats hell out of Earls Court, eh? (*To* ANNE) Did you really think I'd die for you? All I had in mind was a little game, to teach you and Widdecombe a lesson, the pleasure of seeing and hearing you recriminating over my corpse, and a little publicity — I did 'phone the T.V. people by the way, I was going to rise up before them and announce our divorce, how typical of them to pass me over yet again — and then I was going to walk with dignity out of your life, perhaps even into a bit of real telly work on the strength of my little self-promotion — but real killing — real death —

ANNE (*to* HERMAN). You fool! Didn't you look properly! Don't you know the only thing he can do is blood and falling about and pretending to be dead. I told you often enough.

ROBERT. Do you really prefer Brucie's homicidal brother to me! How you've hated me then.

ANNE. From the first time you betrayed me. Everything I said Widdecombe said about our marriage was true. And I knew you'd make a misery of my life once the time was come to throw you out — and I was right, you have. You would! And now you're standing there looking self-righteous — you who screwed all the girls —

HERMAN. Three hundred and fifty seven, Robert. Widdecombe's got it on tape see. (*He shows him the tape-recorder.*) So nothing's really changed, apart from your being alive that is. You're still through.

ROBERT. I never betrayed you. Not once. A dab of lipstick on an item of laundry, an occasional bath, telephone conversations which were what I didn't want them to seem — to you — and what was worst of all you never bothered even to notice. As far as I could tell. This is very humiliating, in front of Brucie's homicidal brother but I loved her, yes and was happy looking after her and her monstrous ego and her merely average talent, yes I was, but I did now and then want you to care, you see, to show a little courteous jealousy — I knew perfectly well that my only real gifts were a stage-manager's gifts, and how could I spend the rest of my life being a stage-manager when the woman I adored made us so rich that *my* pay was simply a tax burden, what was the point? So if I was happy enough running the house while you were out rehearsing, and cooking you special little meals at night when you came back exhausted from your triumphs, I still wanted you to believe that I had some value to others — three hundred and fifty seven others, which were my three hundred and fifty seven failed attempts to get you to see it — (*During this he has sat down at the desk, and is doing something to the gun, very deftly, but looking at them, as he speaks.*) — oh, and what about your Gris. What had you planned for her.

HERMAN. There wasn't any Gris. Apart from Annie.

ROBERT. Ah, just a way of handing over gun and knife, eh?

HERMAN. That's right, Robert. But it was quite instructive, listening to your advice to go ahead and take her from her husband, remember?

ROBERT (*is now dialling on the telephone*). Hello, can I speak to Fred Widdecombe, please. Oh, is that Rosie, hello Rosie, this is a colleague — of your husband's. Would you please tell him that Robert Simon 'phoned, as right as rain, that it was all a joke and that he's absolutely in the clear whatever he hears, he's not involved. O.K.? And give him my — my regards. And to Nigel and Piers — oh, by the way, try one of the elocution classes in the acting schools for Nigel's stammer, they're quite good at that, goodbye, (*Hangs up.*)

HERMAN. The police will be here any moment, they'll give you a bollocking —

ROBERT. I didn't call them, Herman. You did.

HERMAN. Anyway, you can piss off now, man. And you won't be getting any five thousand, even. Will he, Annie?

ANNE. Oh, you two can sort it out between you, I've got my half to make, you know, and you've put me in a dreadful state, damn you, all for nothing.

HERMAN. What do you mean, Annie, what half?

ROBERT. She's got to be in the theatre half an hour before the curtain goes up. She's not with you or me, you know, she's already in the theatre. You wouldn't have lasted with her seven days — let alone seven years. Not once you'd done her job for her.

HERMAN. I'll come with you Annie — and you'd better be gone when we get back.

ROBERT. Just a minute. (*He points the gun at them.*)

HERMAN. Oh come on, man, they're blanks. Annie —

ROBERT. *Don't* call her Annie, if you please. Especially in that accent. They're not blanks. I've just put your bullets back in. This time I'm going to do it right — come here, darling.

ANNE *doesn't move.*

HERMAN. Better do what he says, Annie.

ROBERT. Get the knife, Herman.

HERMAN. What?

ROBERT. Get the knife.

HERMAN *gets the knife.*

ROBERT. Back to the beginning. A knife and a loaded gun in a multi-potential situation. It could come out any way. You've got ten seconds, darling, (*Moving himself to stand with his back to* HERMAN) and then I fire. Last words, please? One — two — three —

ANNE's *lips move desperately.*

ROBERT. Quote then. You've done Cleopatra, Hedda — just a

few lines to exit on. Don't worry about context. Four — five —
six —

HERMAN *creeps across the room.*

ROBERT. — seven eight nine —

HERMAN. Don't!

ANNE *screams.* ROBERT *fires, twice.* HERMAN *plunges the
knife into* ROBERT's *back.* ROBERT *stumbles, points the
gun at* ANNE *again, struggles towards her.* ANNE *grabs the
gun, shoots, as* HERMAN *pulls* ROBERT *back.*

There is a pause. ROBERT *reels away, sits down on the floor.*

ROBERT. Now — now we'll see — how the real process is when —
when there's a knife in my back, Herman, from you and a
bullet in my gut darling from you? — we've got what you
wanted in the end, eh? This is the first death speech I've ever
been allowed to make, and look, I can taste it — real blood —
and when they come tell them — of carnal bloody and
unnatural acts — accidental judgments — casual slaughters, of
deaths put on by cunning and forc'd cause, and in the upshot,
purposes mistook fall'n on the inventor's head — and that
none of it — would have — happened — if it hadn't been —
stage-managed by — by — a — poet — (*He reaches out a hand to*
ANNE, *dies.*)

HERMAN. Jesus. (*Little pause.*) He made us do it — two blanks
and a live bullet — what a bastard!

ANNE. What — what will we do, darling?

HERMAN. Hide him. Quick. Before they come. Where, Annie,
where?

ANNE. In — in the loft.

HERMAN (*picks up the body*). Jes-us!

There is the sound of a car arriving, off, left.

HERMAN. Who is it?

ANNE (*runs to the french windows, looks out*). Kent Television.
They're going round to the front —

There is the sound of a siren in the distance.

HERMAN. Jesus! Quick Annie, open it up. (*He struggles towards the loft ladder with the body.*)

ANNE (*pulls on the rope*). ANNE's *dummy body hurtles down as before.*

ANNE *screams. The sound of the police siren now hideously loud. Ringing on the door off, left, and banging.*

ANNE *continues to scream as:*

Lights.

Curtain

Appendix

[This passage, written during rehearsal, should be incorporated into page 10 after ANNE says: 'A loaded gun?' (line 6). ROBERT's subsequent speech 'Yes, I'll tell you while we're noshing . . .', ending with his going into the kitchen, is cut. The scene resumes where 'ANNE *sits for a moment, then takes out a cigarette* . . .' (line 12.]

ANNE. A loaded gun?

ROBERT. With real bullets.

ANNE. And Herman pointed it at you?

ROBERT. Indeed.

ANNE. Why?

ROBERT. Ah. Well let me break his confidence properly while we're noshing. It deserves a bit of scene-laying and tension-building. I'll be putting it on the table in (*Looks at his watch*) five minutes, I promise — so, in the mean time you settle yourself with this — (*Hands her the drink*) — and I'll dispose of the day's little businesses. (*He goes to the desk, picks up a sheet of paper.*) Phone calls. Paddy, just after you'd left, to ask whether you'd looked at it. I said no, but I'd had a little dip myself and had to say I couldn't imagine you wanting to do a musical. Even of *Miss Julie.* He's going to 'phone again over the weekend. Then Janie 'phoned, wanting to know when you're going to pick up those three scripts or should she send them, there's one she thinks you might find quite exciting, I couldn't get much out of her except that as it stands you'd be playing an eighteen year old. (*He looks at her.*)

ANNE (*abstracted*). Mmmm?

ROBERT. You'd be playing an eighteen year old.

ANNE. Oh. (*Little pause.*) What at?

ROBERT (*laughs*). But if the author knows you're interested he'd re-write it for a twenty-eightish to thirty-sevenish year old — anyway, she wants you to read it quickly, so we

finally worked out that she'll drop it at the stage door
tomorrow, and post the other two — now — oh Patty yes —
(*He looks at her.*) Head, neck, or shoulders?

ANNE. What? Oh — a — a slight head-ache —

ROBERT. And on an empty stomach. Quick. (*Comes around
the back of her, and puts his thumbs on the back of her neck.*)

ANNE. No — it's not that sort of ache.

ROBERT. Still, a few minutes of thumb-work never does you any
harm — (*He begins to knead, glancing down at the note as he
does so.*) Yes, Patty, *three* calls from Patty, actually, about
my proposed emendations to that bloody American interview,
I finally succeeded in explaining to her why she had to
explain to them why we objected to our home being
described as rural-bijou and our life-style as humdrum — I
also got her to get them to get my name right, they still had
me in as Robert Roberts — but that's all sorted out now,
subject to a final check on the proofs and — your approval
of the photograph, they want to use that one taken in
Antibes last year, only with me cut out, which I don't
at all mind, especially as they're titling the piece 'The
Lonely Queen of the London Stage', and I wouldn't want
people to think they meant me, especially as I'm leering
over your shoulder like a drunken lesbian, bad for both our
images, as Patty pointed out, although of course there are
some perfectly decent photographs of the two of us
somewhere about, I suppose. Mmmm? Ah, there's a knot —
(*Working hard with his thumbs*) — what do you think?

ANNE. Mmmmm?

ROBERT. About their using the Antibes photograph?
(*Stopping the massage.*)

ANNE. Oh. Fine. Fine.

ROBERT. It wouldn't be a sympathetic twosome, just of you.
As they've cut me out.

ANNE. Oh. Well, you're not really in it, anyway.

ROBERT. No. Right, well, we've cleared that up, then. Though
after dinner we might have a little riffle through the photo

files to see what else we do have. Now let's see — what's this — how's that?

ANNE. Oh. Better. Much better. Thanks.

ROBERT (*smiles at her*). Good. (*He looks at the list.*)
Psychotic nun, psychotic nun, do we know any psychotic nuns? Oh yes, of course, that girl! *Sounded like* a psychotic nun, heavily cultivated working-class accent *and* a peculiar sort of speech defect, said she wanted to speak to you on a really personal matter — weally perthonal matter, actually, which means she's probably W.R.P. and wants you to contribute money or lead a march — unless of course she's merely a psychotic nun — I tried to fob her off but she'll either ring back or probably pester you at the stage door, I expect, we'll have to change our number again — and old Harriet 'phoned, could we have dinner after the show next week, I said conditional on your being up to it, we'd absolutely love to on the further condition that it wasn't at a restaurant with an Irish owner who a) insists on joining us at the table and then b) falls asleep at it with c) his hand in your lap and his hair in my duck, and she said, well, at least he'd torn up the bill and I *didn't* say, knowing how fond of her you sometimes are, that that was no consolation to *us* as *we* hadn't been expecting to pay it anyway, she's going to 'phone on Monday to confirm, and in the meanwhile I hope is working on my hint about our recently revived taste for Chinese food with the opening of that new place behind Covent Garden, and then lastly — what, oh yes, well I won't bore you with an account of my twenty-five minute altercation over the Stilton I sent back, or with my various other altercations with electricity people over the two new plugs they failed to put in last week, etc; — so that's the lot, oh, except for the post, which came at one thirty today, can you believe, and which divides itself into the two usual piles —

A bell rings from kitchen.

Ah, ready! — fan letters and bills. (*He goes quickly to the desk, picks up a very large pile, hands it to* ANNE) so why don't you look through the fans while I toss the salad —

oh, oh sorry darling, wrong way around, those are the bills —
these (*Picking up the very small pile*) are the fans — not the
usual proportions I know, a lot of things have come in
together, but we'll go through them on Sunday, shall we,
there are one or two items that might seem a little bizarre
at first glance — (*Taking the large pile back*) these are the
fans (*Handing her the small pile*) oh, but not that one, or
that one, both written by the same person, I suspect, and
drunk at the time, anyway if he's so keen to get his money
back he should have applied to the box-office — but the
other two (*Handing them back*) are very charming, in their
simple-minded way. Now for the salad. (*He bustles off to
the kitchen.*)

ANNE *tosses the letters down. Sits for a moment, then
takes out a cigarette . . .*